Strategic Data Management for Successful Healthcare Outcomes

Strategic Data Management for Successful Healthcare Outcomes

Hema Lakkaraju

BEP
BUSINESS EXPERT PRESS
Leader in applied, concise business books

Strategic Data Management for Successful Healthcare Outcomes

First published in 2021 by
Business Expert Press, LLC
222 East 46th Street, New York, NY 10017
www.businessexpertpress.com

ISBN-13: 978-1-63742-149-9 (paperback)
ISBN-13: 978-1-63742-150-5 (e-book)

Business Expert Press Healthcare Management Collection

Collection ISSN: 2333-8601 (print)
Collection ISSN: 2333-861X (electronic)

First edition: 2021

10 9 8 7 6 5 4 3 2 1

Dedicated to my family

Description

Strategy is paramount for successful modern healthcare data management.

The healthcare landscape continues to evolve in an effort to accommodate our ever-connected world. A digital healthcare system poses new challenges and exposes existing issues as professionals—like you—strive to solve concerns. This book recognizes the unique tasks of dedicated professionals while attempting to decrease confusion on this key topic.

It's time to discuss why strategy is important for modern healthcare data management, how strategy can create new business or upscale a business in healthcare data management, and how these tactics assist your business in gaining a competitive advantage.

Cut through the frustration generated by the staggering amount of healthcare data currently being created, collected, and distributed—this book will teach you how.

This book will help you to understand:

- Critical types of data
- How to strategically manage data
- How to build better patient care
- Tips for improving performance
- New ways for your business to thrive

And so much more…

Keywords

healthcare; digital health; big data; strategy; healthcare data management; startups; ethics; pandemic healthcare management; data management

Contents

Testimonials

"Hema Lakkaraju has written this important work to describe the imperative for strategic data management in modern healthcare. This book not only describes how to navigate healthcare data management, but also how to thrive while immersed in these data so that the reader can deliver the highest possible value and impact to their organizations, patients, and to the overall healthcare ecosystem."—**Dan Weaver, *Co-Founder and CTO | Swellter, Inc.***

"Applying a data-centric architecture is mandatory for any organization planning to use data to improve patient outcomes while respecting data privacy. This book sheds light on its importance, impact, and its application."
—**Dan Demers, Co-Founder and CEO at Cinchy; President, Data Collaboration Alliance**

Foreword

We live in wondrous times, ripe with possibilities for using rapid technological evolution to improve the number of healthy years lived by all humanity. In this innovatively dynamic and increasingly integrated world of modern healthcare we must pause to consider one aspect in particular: how and where to begin sifting, sorting, and understanding healthcare data?

With adoption and adaptation of existing and emerging technologies, integration across technical solutions and healthcare environments, and strategic partnerships among stakeholders, the healthcare industry is attempting to provide a complete digital health ecosystem. The bigger question now becomes how to aggregate and manage these vast volumes of healthcare data in a meaningful manner—seeking and garnering insights that add quality years of life for everyday people. At Swellter we're grappling with these challenges on behalf of cancer patients, but that is only one important aspect of the need.

Hema Lakkaraju has written this important work to describe the imperative for strategic data management in modern healthcare. This book describes not only how to navigate healthcare data management, but also how to thrive while immersed in the data so that the reader can deliver the highest possible value and impact to their organizations, patients, and the overall healthcare ecosystem.

—Dan Weaver, Cofounder and CTO | Swellter, Inc.

Acknowledgments

As this book comes to the forefront for a wide audience to read, I would like to express my gratitude and thank a few people who have made this possible for me.

First in line to thank would be Roger Santos for his inspiration. Santos has been involved for 30 years in technical and managerial roles within IT systems and communication technologies and 17 years in management for healthcare technology solutions with a breadth of diverse organizational responsibilities.

Second, I would like to thank Pawan Kohli for his guidance, thoughts, and experience that helped me put this book together. Kohli is a health tech executive, transformation leader, and program director.

I would then like to express my utmost gratitude to Dan Weavers who has been a key source of motivation for me to put this book together. Weaver has been in leadership roles leading operations for some of America's largest health organizations. He is also a thought leader in healthcare data privacy and security.

My acknowledgments would remain incomplete without mentioning the influence of Matthew Taylor and Gil Bashe. Matthew Taylor, who is a Vice President in Solutions at NextGen Healthcare, where his specialty lies in population health, health IT and has vast, intriguing experience at many other large organizations. Taylor has 15+ years of experience in the healthcare sector and has had the privilege of leading data and technology groups at the executive level at nationally recognized provider and health plan organizations. Bashe, on the other hand, has been tapped by PharmaVOICE "as one of the 100 most inspiring people in healthcare"; included in the Fast Company "50 People to Watch in the New World of Work"; chosen as an MM&M Top 10 Innovation Catalyst; chosen by PRWeek/MM&M as a "Top 50 Health Influencer"; noted by Medium's Medika Life as a "Top 50 Healthcare Influencer"; and recognized by the PRSA Health Academy with its "Excellence in Public Relations" award,

PM360 with its "Trailblazer Lifetime Achievement Award," and selected for the PR News "Hall of Fame."

A couple of inspirational figures for this book would be Hans Keil, Dan Demers, Chris McLellan, and Levi Shapiro. Keil has led IT departments for many big health and life science organizations. At present, he is IT executive for one of the largest healthcare systems in United States. His strategic thinking has transformed IT into an efficient and high-performing department in many organizations. Demers is the CEO and cofounder of Cinchy, a pioneer in Data Fabric and Dataware technology. He is also president of Data Collaboration Alliance nonprofit (datacollaboration.org). McLellan is a growth marketer, category designer, and community builder who specializes in the advancement of leading-edge technologies. He is currently focused on advancing technologies related to data ownership and inclusive innovation at the Data Collaboration Alliance nonprofit (datacollaboration.org). Shapiro is a digital health technology innovator with a successful track record of launching new companies and investments.

I would like to also thank Adam Samson and Albert Di Rienzo. Di Rienzo is an accomplished executive and innovator with broad experience in scientific, technologic, and business leadership. Samson has over a decade of experience in clinical research spanning multiple domains. He began his career working directly with patients and transitioned into clinical operations and project management roles of increasing responsibility within CROs, academia, pharma, and tech.

I would also like to thank physicians: Dr. Pitta, Dr. Thota, and Dr. Konidena for sharing their insights on the present challenges' doctors face with respect to health data management.

Last but not the least, I would like to thank my friends and family for always being around and their unconditional support in making this book happen.

Introduction

In this ever-changing and increasingly integrated world of modern healthcare, one wonders where to start and how to understand the healthcare data.

With adaptability of technology, integration, and strategic partnerships, healthcare is attempting to provide a digital healthcare ecosystem. The bigger question is how to manage the healthcare data during this fast digitalization.

Modern healthcare is changing rapidly. Healthcare is hugely digitalized and integrated more than ever before. One hopes that this will solve these problems, but it sometimes increases the confusion.

There is a considerable amount of frustration, confusion mounting up in patients and healthcare organizations with the gigantic amount of health data created, collected, and distributed.

It is so crucial to introduce the concept and methodology of strategic and lean data management and how one can incorporate it in modern healthcare. This will help teams and leadership build smart and sustainable healthcare.

More importantly, this book helps you to understand critical types of data, how to strategically manage it to build better patient care and improve performance. With this book I want to introduce, motivate, stimulate, and inspire you to lead data management in a smart and strategic way. This approach will bring innovative ways for your business to thrive, increase your performance, and greatly improve the care for every patient.

CHAPTER 1

Modern Healthcare

Health data has taken multiple forms over years. Its importance and impact are undeniable over thousands of years.

History of Healthcare Data Management (HDM) Transformation

Data record keeping for healthcare is not a modern concept. Health records have been found on clay tablets inscribed with the ancient language of cuneiform conveying patient information to keep a record of the patient condition and treatment given. These records date back about 5,000 years to the Mesopotamians. The Egyptians continued this data record-keeping process for thousands of years transcribed on papaya for patient care tracking and condition evaluation for future medical reference. These records were safe from misuse as only learned professionals could read and write so the security and privacy of a patient at these times was not a concern.

Fast forward 2,000 years, and the process of healthcare record keeping was the same as the Egyptians: Now records were kept on paper in file folders in file cabinets in siloed doctors' offices and hand carried between different providers keeping the records safe but having limited benefit to the healthcare community. The jump from clay tablets, papaya, and paper to globally networked digital database servers housing electronic health records (EHRs) did not come until very recently in this healthcare record-keeping timeline. In the 1960s the idea of adding additional information to help track the life cycle of the patient so that others could pick up the care and treatment with a full understanding of the patient's history and response to care came into play. Up until this time, healthcare records usually recorded only the diagnosis and the treatment provided.

The concept and reason behind healthcare record keeping had not changed over the years but with the newly formed concept of the "problem-oriented" record keeping, healthcare records would change adding supplemental information that would form the foundation of modern data sets, and those data sets would begin to play a big role in the coming record-keeping revolution. This would also introduce some concerns around the security of the patient information, as illiteracy was no longer a safeguard.

Once this concept of problem-oriented record keeping was introduced the idea was that preventative action could be taken as you now had cause, treatment, and effect forming the first data points in healthcare record keeping and those data points could be compared to other patients for improved outcomes. The new data points were proving helpful in preventative medicine but the access to the records and the cross-referencing of patient records for researchers was simply too difficult for practical outcome gains. The use of digitally stored data made it easier to look at and extract useful data and the advantage of storing records in an electronic format made the storage and retrieval of the records easier but the full conversion to digital records for every patient away from paper would take a few more years.

The recognition behind the value of electronic records was driven by the need for greater efficiency of access to the data collection, the volume of the potential data, and the potential for positive patient outcomes from that data analyses. The development of an EHR database improved the patient health record data collection, storage, access, and cross-referencing, which were made easier by an order of 100× magnitude. Now healthcare had the ability to cross-reference all aspects of a patient's medical encounters with great specificity and compare conditions, cause, treatment, and outcomes to improve outcomes for the broader population. The limiting factor in this revolution of healthcare record keeping was that the information on patients was kept on server databases isolated to the institution providing care for those patients.

The next step was to expand the access to the records for a broader cross-section of patients from around the world.

Well, the computational world is moving quickly toward the use of quantum bit processors for processing the vast amounts of data that have been compiled in healthcare databases around the world. And because of the development of quantum computing (QC), the quantum key distribution (QKD) encryption model is necessary. Securing the data of the communication becomes more difficult. The very thing that makes the QC so valuable to healthcare makes it a threat to healthcare. The quantum computing (QC) can not only improve outcome for medical diagnostics, but also be used to break the longest encryption strange available by a binary processor in a matter of seconds rendering the encryption of the data useless. The value quantum bit processing brings to healthcare initially takes the form of an improved provider medical resource for diagnosing and treating patients. Data processing request from a practitioner concerning the diagnosing of a condition and determining the best course of action for treatment takes time, and in some cases, the patient does not have the luxury of time. A quantum computer can process all the data available in the world and return an assessment to the provider in a matter of seconds as opposed to several minutes or even hours depending on the data set query. Researchers can use extensive and seemingly disjointed data queries and produce previously unimagined data results advancing preventative healthcare initiatives on orders of magnitude in minutes or hours instead of weeks and months.

Roger Santos' interview shares above glimpse of the past, present, and future of healthcare.

At present, in this fifth industrial revolution, innovation is occurring with an inclusion of people and machines. Fifth industrial revolution brought in the need and want for personalized healthcare by people. This need can be performed successfully through strategic data management.

It is very clear that technology and tools changed more frequently yet data at the core and its value are irreplaceable. It is very important to create a health data management which can provide high value and performance beyond technology changes.

The Present Healthcare Data and Their Challenges

There are healthcare challenges at present which include adaptability, agility, interoperability, and implementation of these digital technologies in the healthcare system.

Mobile Network Coverage

Mobile health technology can be adopted by people only when they have the basic mobile network coverage. Yet, unfortunately, every one in five Americans living in rural areas lacks mobile phones through which they can go online and access digital facilities. While the number of mobile devices in rural American areas has sharply increased, adults in these areas are still 10 to 12 percent less likely to have a smartphone than in urban or suburban areas.

There are noticeable gaps between the network usage of rural versus urban American populations alone, making one wonder about the status of other nations.

Mobile network coverage is a big feature in adopting mobile health technology. Without it, a digital healthcare system is hard to imagine. Many major organizations, nowadays, are allying to improve the situation. The Federal Communications Commission is on phase II of its Connect America Fund, a plan to expand broadband access and mobile coverage for rural communities in the United States [1]. These efforts will need to be consistent if progress is to be expected on any digital fronts. It might take some time for the rural area to be fully functional and take full advantage of the mobile health products.

Expanding the footprint of the mobile network might bring more adaptability for mobile health as it has become the core necessity during the current pandemic and for the future as well.

The need for such technology and network was made apparent with the emergence of the COVID-19 worldwide pandemic. A greater collaboration was needed between countries to research the virus and get a vaccine created in time. The virus strand was new, and information was needed to better understand it: how it affects people, the levels of severity in the affected, its cure, and what can be done to avoid it. Digitalization was instrumental in our fight against the pandemic, providing the tools to share massive volumes of medical data across distances and process valuable insights out of them. It also opened the possibility of remote medical assistance, reducing some of the risks for frontline medical workers.

Yet, it is worth noting that digital health innovation was already making unmatched progress even before the pandemic. With a range of products, mobile apps, telehealth, telemedicine, and more, the pace at which innovations are being made projected a sum close to $207 billion in investment by the year 2026 [2].

Internet Access

While the dwellers of cities and metropolitans have taken the speed and availability of our Internet connections for granted, it is not the same for everyone around the world. In urban centers, the provision of Internet connections and broadband is present and being used for a plethora of purposes such as telecommunication, data storage, data sharing, and a constant exchange of information, but things are different in the rural and underdeveloped areas.

While our digital health products function seamlessly, rural areas are far behind in this walk toward a more sophisticated future. According to data from the Federal Communications Commission, 39 percent of people living in rural areas in the United States lack access to high-speed broadband [3]. It is a significant percentage: Almost half of the rural population is without the necessity for making up the foundation of a digital healthcare system. Considering the lack of what is an essential resource in a population this big, it becomes difficult to imagine a complete transition to digital. Hospitals and clinics cannot, as a result, maximize the usage of the digital health products devised with such zeal and fervor in these rural areas.

Low Internet penetration remains a key issue of healthcare in this digital era. If progress must be made on a broader scale and with the inclusion of all populations, urban and rural, then the issue of Internet access would have to be solved beforehand and with efficiency.

Data Centricity

While the world is producing data on all fronts, in ever-increasing quantities, and is coming up with more digital health products, services, and management tools than ever before, we need ways and resources to share this data on a central server to benefit one another and enhance efficiency. In the healthcare sector, data comprises lab results, genomics data, vital signs, medications, medical images, and more. It has accumulated into a tremendous amount in total. Around 25 exabytes (1 exabyte = 1 billion gigabytes) worth of medical data is present to date.

Dan Demers, entrepreneur, and successful IT executive, explains the present data management challenges and how data centricity can bring value. Health data sets are from different sources and are often siloed. These siloed datasets from multiple systems raise the concerns around sharing and collaboration. The traditional approach of sharing includes data copies or duplicates into other systems. This can bring in the control and security issues.

Data centricity can:

• Reduce the operation cost and time for multiple systems
• Provide clear visibility of data from multiple sources

Collaboration is the key and need. In healthcare, collaboration is under scrutiny due to its privacy and security concerns. Modern governance includes data centricity which can enhance safe and secure data-centric collaboration efforts at a global scale.

Centralized data can open the doors to understanding health data better, create a smart health ecosystem, and create patient-centric healthcare as information would be dispersed and deployed.

To create a safe, secure, smart, and sustainable healthcare ecosystem, healthcare needs a clear sense of the idea of health data with respect to the patient. This becomes a big challenge if data is sprawled and scattered. Creating a centralized patient-centric health data system thus becomes the foundation for delivering excellent healthcare. This scattered data can be gathered via centralization. In addition, more tools and data-centralizing platforms need to be made for better data management.

SaaS platforms, tools, and apps that can help us with medical data processing are already present, but the issue is that they do not gather all the information present in one place. This potentially results in data sprawling. Data sprawling is another term for scattered data in multiple systems. Data sprawling creates new challenges, especially in visible patient data. As healthcare and patients are starting to generate more and more data from digital health products and services, there is a greater need to bring it all into one place. The challenges around data visibility and management also need to be met head-on.

Legacy and Siloed Data Systems

In an interview, Pawan Kohli explains that in most of the cases about the systems and infrastructures, many local and mid-sized hospitals are still running on older systems which might be missing several things or might just not have the budget as well as the resources to upgrade. The systems are old, there are various system compatibility issues, and the understanding of health IT systems is weak with little patient privacy. It is not that there is trouble with patient privacy, but a lack of the infrastructure involved could lead to a leak in patient privacy.

Another problem that comes up is the fact that the systems are not just extremely old but have tech systems in miserable conditions, and in some cases, completely nonexistent. The systems are also not integrated and rather detached from one another, unlike the desired interoperability. These systems need to be replaced, and that must be the final step into this roadmap as a new, digitized healthcare system evolves and doesn't just evolve, but becomes an essential part of how healthcare operates, is viewed, and wonders in many ways.

When physicians Dr. Pitta, Dr. Thota, and Dr. Konidena were interviewed, it was clear that there are still challenges that are unanswered:

- For small- and mid-sized hospitals, interoperability is still a challenge. The efficiency and poor interface demand more time for clinical-type data entry and takes valuable time from patient care. This can lead to poor satisfaction for patients and physicians.
- There is still room for improving efficiency in terms of interoperability and integrating technology platforms.
- In big hospitals, physicians are bombarded with more administrative work and more health data access which are not always useful. These again effect patient satisfaction.

Proper Use of Technology

Hans Keil, an IT executive, shared his view on the present challenges regarding technology fit in modern healthcare management ecosystem. There are big solutions and tools that are used by hospitals that remain in an immature state as of now. The solutions, he further believes, need to be evolved to understand the data better from the huge data pool.

Even though there has been a great improvement of new Artificial Intelligence tools which look for anonymous behavior of data pools for security purposes, there is still an unclear definition of data criticality and risk. At present, hospitals are getting sunk from the data well. This data well is coming from multiple unique sources like medical devices, clinical trials, applications, and hospital systems.

Among these, he argues, at the highest level remains the ever so big challenge of centralized data. It is also important to note, according to him, that health IT departments in hospitals are looking for suboptimized multilayer interoperability, which makes things slightly more complicated; the strategic data approach is less in the workforce at present.

He goes on to argue that the scale of efforts to bring in data management is huge. This includes but is not limited to resources, roles, and mainly process.

Pandemic Healthcare Data

However, the pace might have been greatly accelerated due to the needs of a world ridden by COVID-19. In dealing with the virus, rapid progress is currently being made in many research areas, including modes of sharing data and methods of enhancing deep learning for COVID-19. Improved deep learning models can help us in a range of medical applications. For instance, they can help us more accurately read x-ray images to tell COVID-19 patients apart from pneumonia patients and more.

There is still a tremendous untapped potential regarding the utilization of digital health products. This potential needs to be explored if the medical industry is truly to benefit from the digital revolution.

Healthcare has come a long way in digital health innovation from when it started 5,000 years ago and still has a long way to go. Now, the question is not about how healthcare needs to assess digital health as a silo problem but how it should build a smart health ecosystem to bring together all that it has present now. If healthcare succeeds in creating a strategic data management system, it would be able to build a stronger patient-centric, fast-performing, and customized smart healthcare ecosystem.

While all the technologies are effortlessly built all around, the consumers of data too are increasing at an astonishing rate. It wouldn't come as a surprise that there is a huge need for data strategy here, which can not only support but thrive business decisions but also be compliant with regulations.

CHAPTER 2

The Critical Role and Value of Data

Data is what defines a unique individual, organization, or service provider. It is all the information available on and provided by these three. Data can be of any kind: consumer data of an e-commerce website to learn buyer patterns; user data on gaming consoles to track status and progress of gamers in their plays; or patient data in healthcare systems recorded by collecting test results, reports, and expenditures on medicine.

Data is everywhere, from your workplace to the streaming site you watch movies to the grocery shop you visit every month to the clinic you get your routine tests from. Organizations collect data on people to use it for future advancement of their services and other purposes like advertisement and intelligence. Vast amounts of data make up big data. Big data is a term used to refer to a bulk of data. While companies are collecting, using, and running on data these days, they are also working toward managing this data and decluttering it for efficient usage. Data management has become a business currently. Companies work solely to make something useful out of hundreds of data sets for further usage by AI scientists.

Big data can be transformed to benefit many facets of industries, including the healthcare industry. It can be used to spread awareness, support the research already being done, support service providers, and make more information for comprehension of patterns.

In healthcare, big data comes from several sources, as indicated in Figure 2.1.

Healthcare big data is driven from payer records, smartphones, wearable devices, search engine data, public records, EHR, and so on. In an age of ever-expanding digitalization, it is only appropriate and efficient to store the information collected to build intelligent machines that can

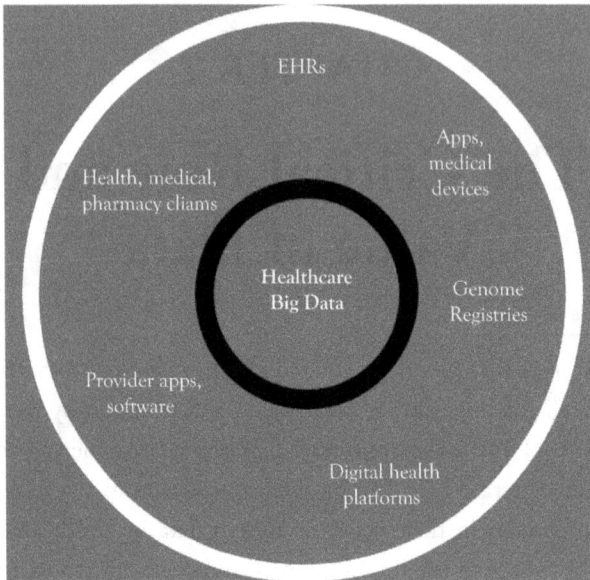

Figure 2.1 Healthcare big data

learn and apply, helping users and customers take precautions and cura-tive measures. Modern healthcare data is an accumalation of data coming from multiple sources as mentioned in Figure 2.1.

The kinds of data taken from the different sources are also of various types. Some are collected from remote monitoring devices that routinely pick up information on patients, some are from the personal patient data, and some are direct outcomes of electronic medical record (EMR) feeds and abstract. The following data usage by organizations helps us under-stand the patterns of data collection and the many types of it as part of big data: Most organizations use EMR abstracts, claims data, and enrollment data in risk adjustment, quality ratings, and care management, while few utilize patient lifestyle information and survey data for these same causes and purposes.

The benefits of HDM are numerous. Among the most notable include the following:

• A comprehensive understanding of patient groups and house-holds is key to predict diseases and learn status.

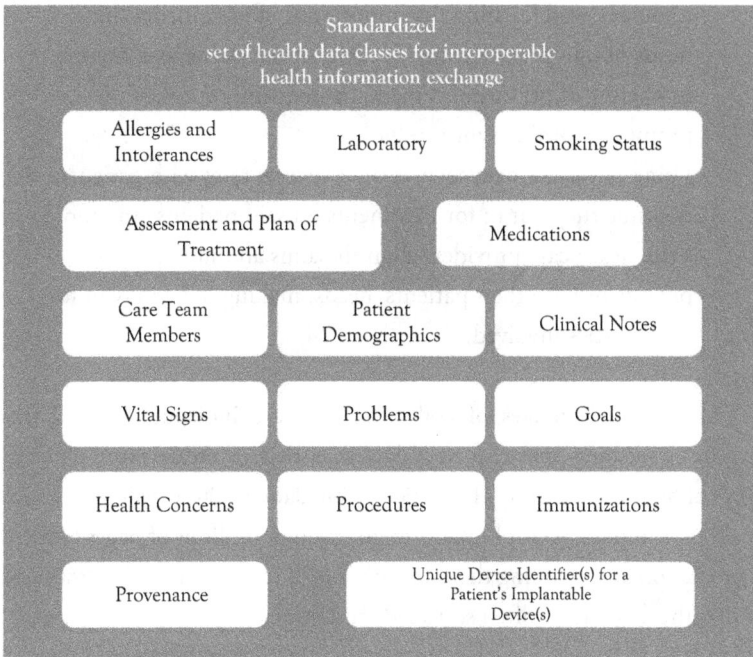

Figure 2.2 Standardized set of health data classes for interoperable health information exchange [4]

Reference: United States Core Data for Interoperability (USCDI)

- Patient–doctor engagement is improved by staying up to date with their profiles; it is easier for healthcare professionals to target reminders for them and suggest methods of care.
- Health outcomes are improved, due to the mix of patient profiles and care management: A pattern can be traced of disease spread in a certain population; new trends can be learned, providing time and opportunity for a timely response.
- Synergized standardized health data classes among multiple Health IT platforms minimizes errors and maximizes healthcare performance. Figure 2.2 shows standardized set of health data classes for interoperable health information exchange. Guidance like these can help healthcare organizations create, monitor, and manage synergized health data management.
- This type of data also helps businesses make proactive decisions in recruiting healthcare workers, attaining sufficient

resources, and learning the importance of prioritizing the needs of one patient group over the other. Better and smarter marketing efforts are also made consequently for the promotion of the right product.

- Using physician data such as their success rates with patients, the time they put in for treatments on said patients, and more help, healthcare providers align the aims and milestones of physicians with their patients' needs, making it a win–win for both parties involved.

All these advantages of collecting data are indisputable, and this feature is pushing scientists and data scientists to create more efficient ways of handling all of it. The upside of big data is that it is all digital, not making it impossible for humans to go through millions of pages to form a prediction and enabling them to gather it all in one place. The downside is that this big data is often scattered, and not enough is invested in managing it to form data sets and for machine learning objectives.

The challenges that present health data management face can be categorized into five main types:

- **Diversity in health file types**: Data of any kind is not built, used, and stored in one format. Most of the data in one field is fragmented, being in many different forms. MRI scans are used in DICOM format, for example, and written documents are scanned to be saved. Further variation in format may be in the form of images, videos, spreadsheets, and typed documents. Furthermore, these formats may be replicated and repeated, making it confusing for the system to predict patient behavior. With this duplicity of sources, there exists a lack of surety on the authenticity of data being used, stored, and referred to.
- **Constant evolution**: A set of recorded data may not always remain the same. For example, a patient may provide a record of his or her healthcare decisions steadily, but he or she may go through personal changes such as getting married or changing their address. With their changed lifestyles, their

medications and treatment patterns may also alter, creating bulky layers of new data for the healthcare professional to sift through.

- **Extreme accumulation of data:** It is now believed that more healthcare data collection is better. This brings in the challenges of data storage and reviewing the huge sets of healthcare data with no idea of what is required and how it can be used.

- **Sensitivity and privacy**: Healthcare data is sensitive, to say the least. It is not a small thing to store scores of patients' data; great measures of safety and security must be taken to ensure protection from thieves and hackers. The U.S. Health Insurance Portability and Accountability Act (HIPAA) requires that this data be handled responsibly. Further audits and regulatory concerns make it difficult for the data to be used as freely as it ideally should be. The diversity of application is thus limited, and patient benefits are too, consequently.

- **Silo regulations and standards:** With the present increased landscape of regulations like GDPR and CCPA, it is becoming very clear that personal identifiable information's (PII) safety and security is very important for nations. This also brings in a challenge for organizations on how to implement these effectively on the huge data sets held by an organization.

These five challenges, if dealt with efficiently, can pave the way for smarter usage of big health data.

Healthcare Data Management (HDM) is a valuable tool in revolutionizing the face of healthcare systems in the present and future. The volume, velocity, and value of data are growing exponentially every day. This presents data scientists and data management businesses with not just more to deal with but also more opportunities of making something useful out of the scattered data being stored on cloud servers and other systems by the many hospitals, clinics, private practitioners, institutes, and organizations.

Support in decision making, development of vaccines by timely predictions of epidemics, remote monitoring, and computing large amounts of information are only a few advantages of health data management. It is a valuable business to oversee in this age of cutting-edge technology.

New approaches to health data management are an emerging and highly profitable market. This market has a bright future of solving the biggest challenges from global collaboration to healthcare data synergizing during a pandemic.

Overall, retrieval, analysis, comparison, and output judgment of health data management make it a beneficial tool. It is a gift that will keep on giving to the healthcare industry and keep saving lives in the long run. The smarter and faster the data is managed, and in more efficient ways than that which already exists, the more its applications will open in the real field of work. The role of data is critical, to conclude, and its value only increases by the hour.

CHAPTER 3

The Strategic Health Data Mindset

Data is a commodity at present: The bits of information collected from numerous sources in numerous industries are not only used by private organizations but bought, sold, and exchanged. Besides its application in small-scale purposes by single-unit companies, hospitals, and institutes, hordes of data (big data) are used across multiple platforms for mutual benefits. What one company or organization benefits from it can be found in the form of data available in the structure of another company or organization. User privacy is kept in consideration, of course, but it would not be wrong to state that data is now a commodity, much like most of the things in the world that provide the potential of capital generation.

The world is moving toward having a data-driven mindset, and so many health organizations are still conservative in their approach if they are to be a part of this new and cutting-edge data-driven world.

The adaptability of this truth will bring the greatest advantage for organizations. At present, the mindset of health organizations is to think very deeply and hard on systems, platforms, and processes. Understanding data's fundamental nature is a real art and can bring a tremendous amount of clarity, vision, and mission to organizations. However, it is not entirely straightforward, nor is it completely impossible to understand its nature.

Data brings with itself a whole ecosystem, a chain, or an environment of networks and setups that need to be understood if commodified data is to be used wisely and usefully. These ecosystems are a whole system in which data exists as a particular piece, yet it is the most important one. If an organization intends to adopt a data-driven mindset, it is vital they fully understand the whole ecosystem's workings. The secret of understanding the ecosystem is not to understand the systems, platform, and teams only; instead, it is about understanding the data—the core of the ecosystem on which it is built. Both the values go hand in hand and depend upon each other for usage and adaptability.

The data is the force creating the value of the ecosystem, and thus, creating a data-driven model can bring extraordinary results. Business analysts believe that organizations and healthcare systems need to be driven by data to stay relevant for the next decade, at least, until humanity advances further in terms of scientific and record-keeping technology. Forrester Research analysts have found out that organizations using data and insights to drive their future decisions are growing by 30 percent annually and earning in trillions a year [5].

The world has begun and continues to use data to make decisions. It is clear that a data-driven mindset is necessary for a thriving business/system now, and they need data-driven models for this purpose.

Data-Driven Models and Organizations

Data-driven models are methods of decision making based on existing data or datasets. Building on the usability feature, many analysts believe that individual user access to data is key to a business prospering. Data reports that are vague or passed down from untrustworthy sources are risky and not useful. The results produced from individually accessed data, they concur, are more accurate and up to par.

Patient Data-Centric Mindset

In healthcare systems, the models work the same way. Healthcare data needs to be assessed, improved, and shared in a thorough and mindful manner if something needs to be gained from it. The steps to building a strategic patient data-centric health management model are simple and as Figure 3.1 represents all the different steps of building this which can help build patient data-centric mindset.

Need Versus Want

Knowing what you need is the first step to getting it. By narrowing, categorizing, and assessing your or your organization needs, you can

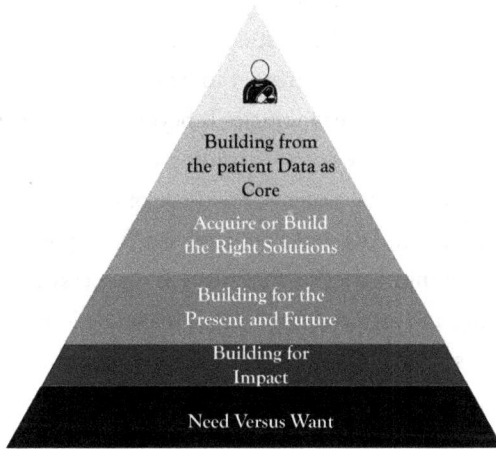

Figure 3.1 Patient data-centric mindset

figure out what and from where you need to access. Building an exceptional service to the patient is possible only after you have recognized the kind of data you require. This recognition takes place because of research and assessment of pre-existing facts present in the form of patient information.

This effort might need a lot of research on understanding the needs of patients. This kind of service is not of the reactive kind but instead proactive, in that it requires advanced work beforehand and in accordance with timeliness.

Data's true value lies in it enabling organizations to proactive health services and helping patients reduce or avoid the health risks like pandemics and serious diseases. The data and its usage are no good for patients if not utilized in time.

Building for Impact

Data has an impact. The impact varies based on what kind of data and how it is used. The best examples of it are the recent ways in which it is used by healthcare organizations to tackle the coronavirus pandemic. The effect of collected data upon the response of hospitals and healthcare personnel was immense. The status of patients signing in, the statistics of recovery ratio, the social distancing patterns studied through geospatial technology, the testing capacities, the extent of people who regularly wore masks all came to describe the existing conditions of the pandemic and build upon the needs and measures yet to be taken.

The impact of modern technologies is beyond doubt: The use of sensory nodes in numerous devices for reading external conditions for the safeguarding of the internal systems, the usage of the readings from those sensors to create sets of data and then applying the reports of data hence created to make things better in the future is a process most impactful. Machine learning and artificial intelligence make the job of humans simpler and have a stronger impact upon the input of time and energy on our part.

Building for the Present and Future

The current needs of the healthcare system are many. Just like the weather, it needs to be able to predict what is coming. Being prepared for a storm helps in dealing with its outcomes. Likewise, being aware of people's existing health conditions helps prevent and cure their conditions and diseases on time. Healthcare policies change rapidly in some countries, and so if a patient is aware of his or her ongoing health situation, it might help them better in tackling it in the future with or without insurance.

Health information systems are one of the six building blocks of the health system as defined by the World Health Organization. Besides leadership and governance, service delivery, health system financing, health workforce, medical products, vaccines, and technologies, the presence of health information systems is necessary for the record-keeping and data building of all parties and processes involved. These needs are not just limited to the present, as emphasized from the past shortcomings, but also are highly needed for the future.

Success and stability of the healthcare system are contingent upon the health system building blocks as defined by WHO. They, in turn, are contingent upon the usage of data for prediction of and preparation for health concerns. In a nutshell, the building of data-driven models and their integration in data-driven organizations is for both the present and the future, a bright, healthy, and successful one at that.

Build strategic data-driven models for your organization for the present and the future because they have a significant impact.

Acquire or Build the Right Solutions

After understanding the health data types needed for your organization, their risk and impact, the next step is to either acquire or create the right tools to implement the methodology. For example, data is needed for building an updated login system for patients; an understanding of login data would help predict future patient intake and the necessary resources.

This method, the second step in building a data-driven model for a data-driven organization, should have one main goal: Creating unbeatable value for the patients and building, both in the present and for the future. Solutions can be built and acquired through different means. An in-house data analytics team can form reports for employees and workers to refer to while treating patients, or outsourced tools can be implemented for the same purposes.

Building From the Core

Creating a patient data-centric healthcare business/organization is a crucial need at present. Cleaning a wound where it is most receptive to bacteria makes the most sense. Likewise, catering to the needs of those who deserve and require it the most is the smart way to go. Building a patient data-centric model from the core of the process is sensible, and that core lies in the patients, the people who depend upon the healthcare system.

We are now moving from digitized to personalized digital health ecosystems.

Long and Continuous Revenue Generation Through Patient Data-Centric Models

The global big data analytics in the healthcare market was valued at $7.0 billion in 2017. It is expected to generate $22.7 billion in revenue by 2023, exhibiting a CAGR (compound annual growth rate) of 21.8 percent during 2018 through 2023 [6]. Creating a patient data-centric model is a billion-dollar business, the goal of which is to create a smart and sustainable ecosystem. The creation of software, the investment in analytics and data scientists, and so on make up for a big business setting.

Big data analytics alone make up for a big chunk of the big data industry. The global market share for artificial intelligence in healthcare by the year 2016 saw an increase in the personal health area. Artificial intelligence directly relies on data for its functions.

Present healthcare models are siloed and less understood. What healthcare is missing is a predictable model based on the data-driven methodologies, which not only predicts what the immediate need is but what need is continuously evolving.

In the healthcare sector, it means healthy living, predictive diagnosis, diagnostics, and appointments, cures, and follow-ups.

Besides these needs, methods, and necessities of building a data-driven model, it is also essential to know how a system-driven mindset can be dangerous.

Why Is a System-Driven Mindset Dangerous and Expensive?

A midsized healthcare organization X in Silicon Valley spent millions of dollars on system-driven data management. As they brought in more systems and more platforms into use, it became a monumental effort and went beyond their control. They started to have management problems with most and all systems eventually, some of which were not even in use and some were partially used. Further, the visibility of data on the systems has become more unclear and lacked governance. It is only one of the many examples of how this kind of maintenance can drain a business: The investment of workforces to maintain these systems and platforms is far more than the use of the systems.

This approach might have made sense a decade ago, but now it is the most ineffective approach, mainly because the value of the system is unknown. The factors to consider the value of a system or platform are unknown, as opposed to a data-driven defined system.

Model-driven development (MDD) has many downfalls, including the rigidity that restricts your generation of results and makes it difficult to make small changes in the model when needed, its inflexibility, and lack of knowledge about it on the customer's part.

The value of a system is determined by data and not by the organization's department, teams, or customers. The sooner this realization is made, the better organizations will be able to transform their modes of functioning and effectiveness.

Understanding the Core Value of a System Is the Key

Many models would be useless without the integration of data, its assessment, and deployment for accurate durability predictions. Data is the core value of a system. Without data, a system cannot achieve what it can with it.

A team or a department might think that a system is more important than others. Coming out of the grandiosity of the system, a data-defined mindset is a transformational force of leaders and organizations.

The key to a successful healthcare or life science organization needs to be understood and understood very well. To understand the key to a successful organization is by looking at it not by people or product, but by the data it contains. It is the beginning of the system and the very brick that lays the foundation for every other structure that comes after it to complete a system.

An organization that understands the value of data and takes decisions driven by data can help to create patient-centric billion-dollar health businesses. Otherwise, their fate would match that of organization X in Silicon Valley. Timely inclusions of demanded technology show its merit in the form of results.

A data-centric mindset will go a long way into the future in terms of advancement and an increment in patients' average life expectancy as the whole procedure would be expedited using organized data bits. Having a data-centric mindset is crucial in the age of viruses and far-reaching diseases. Businesses, too, cannot make it without data and all its implications.

CHAPTER 4

The Art of Strategy in Data Management

As of present, data management is branded and defined by tools, platforms, and systems that need to be understood in totality for better data governance. In recent times, healthcare has been challenged with patient health information (PHI) and personally identifiable information (PII). The sources of these sets of information are from different domains like medical devices, hospital administration systems, digital applications, telehealth, and many more things that come under the umbrella of healthcare. However, it is integral to remember that measuring strategic data management in terms of systems and sources that you might have would be an inappropriate and incorrect way of measurement.

It is better to understand the process further. The change needs to come from within the organization—from system mindset to data mindset. Data is the central tenant of a system, and it is the importance of data that defines the value of an entire system. This value cannot be defined by a team, department, or person. In all of this, understanding the core is important because determining the data management practices always begins by understanding the goal of the organization itself.

The tools and systems are only part of the solution puzzle when it comes to strategic management. If strategy is the first step, which includes understanding data, it tends to impact a few things rather positively, and these are the following things impacted:

- High business value
- High customer or patient satisfaction
- High savings in operational cost
- High savings in operational time

These factors will move on to change the mindset of thinking and creating the value of a system or process within the organization. The most significant advantage here would be that of high business value. New and imaginative plans of action are starting to show guarantee in conveying better consideration and producing more significant yields. The presence of these models and their underlying triumphs are intelligent of what healthcare has seen in the market lately. Driving associations in the medical care industry are not a substance to just play in appealing portions and markets, however. Instead, they are proactively, and in a general sense, reshaping how the business works and how care is conveyed. While the formula across verticals shifts, basic among these new plans of action is more prominent arrangement of motivations commonly including hazard bearing, better joining of care, and utilization of data and progressed investigation.

The idea of leadership, particularly in the modern era owing to digital and "online" options, in the healthcare industry is challenged in many new ways. A significant portion of this leadership struggles with data management. The point over here is not that these individuals do not know what is happening in the market or what is trending for the most part, but rather that they do not understand its mechanics. These mechanics particularly have to do with data management and its strategic use.

With growing technological advancements like Internet of Things, AI, and machine Learning, different data is generated from different sources and channels.

Strategic data management is managing the healthcare data which brings in high data quality, best data architecture, and appropriate implementation of technology and tools.

There are divisions in the healthcare organizations. These can be profit and nonprofit healthcare organizations. For-profit organizations aim to maximize their profits and improve the profits to shareholders. On the other hand, nonprofit organizations aim to cater to community needs. The revenue that they generate needs to be to fulfill the purpose of providing the community's needs. Both need to implement strategic data management, which involves a more strategic data management approach from the market.

Some of the key factors to consider for strategic health data management are given here.

Data Quality

Data quality is a measure of the condition of data based on factors such as accuracy, completeness, consistency, reliability, and whether it's up to date. Measuring data quality levels can help organizations identify data errors that need to be resolved and assess whether the data in their IT systems are fit to serve their intended purpose.

The emphasis on data quality in enterprise systems in healthcare organizations has increased as data processing has become more intricately linked with business operations. Organizations increasingly use data analytics to help drive business decisions. Data quality management is a core component of the overall data management process, and data quality improvement efforts are often closely tied to data governance programs that aim to ensure data is formatted and used consistently throughout an organization.

A portion of the issues confronted while dissecting big data in healthcare is the absence of advanced data examination, incapable framework, lack of financing, doubt in databases, and reluctance to share data. Protection and security concerns, the absence of data specialists and labor force, and an overall absence of instruments are additional challenges in using the capability of big data. There is a critical need to assemble a culture in medication that incorporates the utilization of data in a commonsense manner, so it doesn't obstruct the improvement of inventive data the executive's arrangements.

Now, on to data quality in healthcare. To be useful, data must be correct, complete, reliable, and accurate. Flawed data leads to errors in decision making, lethal mistakes in patient care (such as diagnosing the wrong patient), skewed numbers in research, and other critical problems. While many healthcare facilities have collected data on patients, they have yet to develop up-to-date systems to maintain the quality of services provided. More importantly, it gives organizations a head start into the data improvement journey. Once the organization understands the problems affecting data quality, they can be in a better position to make necessary amendments, coming up with a more robust data management plan.

Health Data Architecture

Data architecture is the way toward normalizing how associations gather, store, change, disperse, and use data. The objective is to convey critical data to individuals who need it and help them figure it out.

The present-day data architecture configuration guarantees that a very much planned interaction puts business tacticians and specialized aptitude at a similar table. Together, they can figure out what data is expected to drive the business forward, how that data can be sourced, and how it tends to be circulated to give significant data to chiefs. What's driven enormous data into this present reality is the developing impact of the cloud, which gives the sort of quick, simple, and minimal effort versatility that cutting-edge data architecture requires. The cloud likewise permits associations to pool a lot or the entirety of their data in one spot, where preferably one expert adaptation of the data is accessible to all who need it.

The growing amount of data in the healthcare industry has made inevitable the adoption of big data techniques to improve the quality of healthcare delivery. Despite the integration of big data processing approaches and platforms in existing data management architectures for healthcare systems, these architectures face difficulties in preventing emergency cases.

Strategic big data architecture is designed to handle huge amounts of data from multiple sources like medical devices, health apps, EHRs, and clinical trials. This has been pushed to be mostly operational. Health data is transforming in the fifth industrial revolution where personalization and digitalization are integrated. Data architecture is a need which brings in strategy in the form of emotional intelligence and high intellect. This can be reached by truly understanding the data value, risk, and impact toward the patient.

Data Ownership

Data ownership can be defined as the responsibility of data one has in possession. It provides control over the data. Now, the question comes down to how data ownership is looked at particularly in the healthcare sector and how it can be used for the same purpose. This can be looked at in two different ways. The first would be the data ownership of patients, doctors, and everyone involved within the medical staff for better research, marketing, and functioning. Another way that data ownership could particularly be used would be to own data that has been collected by other sources, for example, data collected by a pharmaceutical company or a research lab powered by either the government or any other international organization.

The primary data ownership, however, is regarding the collection of data of medically involved stakeholders on a first-hand basis. Institutions tend to believe that they own patient data because they are the ones who collected it. However, these institutions are just data custodians because the data in its entirety remains the property of the patient. Access to this data requires patient consent, done to restrict the exploitative ability of the "big data," which includes techniques like machine learning, as discussed earlier.

The GDPR, followed by the CCPA have been doing the rounds in the healthcare sector today for patient data versus privacy rights. However, these rights do not shed ample light on data ownership. Either way, the consent of patients, as well as medical professionals, is integral to the success of data ownership in healthcare. More efforts are being put into developing standards and regulations which embrace patient privacy and guideways to create an environment to accelerate innovation.

The art of strategy is now more needed that ever. Strategic health data management is a combination of emotional intelligence, innovation with intellect, and understanding the need of data before managing it.

CHAPTER 5

3S—Foundation Pillars for Strategic Health Data Management

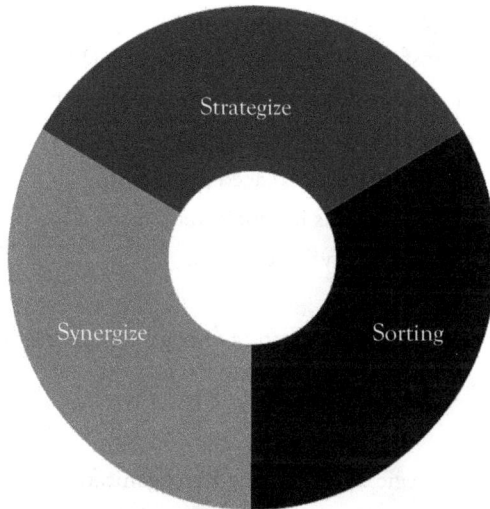

Figure 5.1 3S model of strategic health data management

S—Strategy

Strategic data management is a core requirement for organizations and leaders globally (Figure 5.1). It is a requirement and possibility at present due to the increase in technology and huge amounts of available data. Figure 5.1 potraits the three strong foundational pillars to build strategic health data management: Strategize, Sorting, and Synergize.

From health startups to big healthcare organizations, no organization is the same, no organization pathway is the same. No organization vision and mission is the same. It is the reality and understanding this reality will help organizations understand and create these three unique pillars (Figure 5.1).

When diving into strategic data management, especially for healthcare, the answers to the following questions must be followed through with and ready.

- What kind of organization is yours?
- Where is your organization at present?
- What is the goal of your organization toward patients?
- How is it transformed into data management?
- What is the data handled in the organization at present?
- What data is crucial or high priority?
- How is this crucial data managed at present?
- What is the gap analysis in crucial data management?
- How can this gap analysis be solved?

Figure 5.2 describes the key factors to consider for creating a strategy.

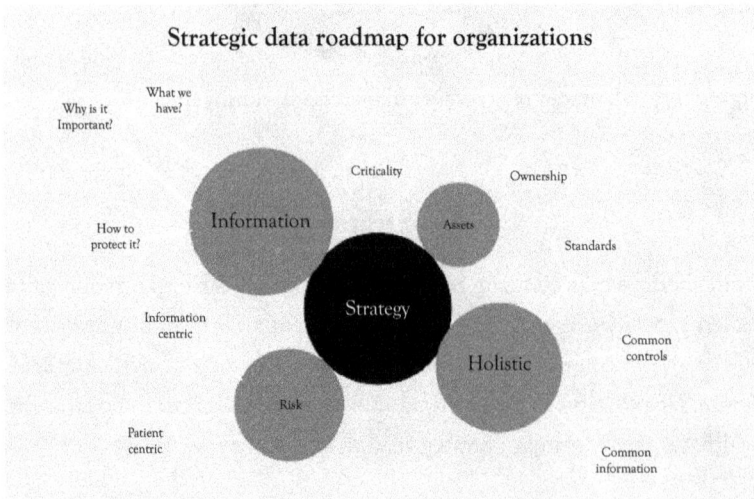

Figure 5.2 Strategic roadmap for organizations

Figure 5.2 describes the four factors which can help build overall strategy for organizations. They are

- Information Strategy
- Risk Strategy
- Assets Strategy
- Holistic Strategy

Information Strategy

Organizations cannot survive without information. It is the life-force of modern organization. Strategy around information can save millions and months for organizations. Information strategy can be built with three questions answered:

- What information does an organization have?
- What set of information is important and why?
- Where is the origin of information (vendor or in-house)?
- How to protect the important information?

Risk Strategy

Organizations need to understand the risks and define their risk appetite. In healthcare organizations, risk can be mainly categorized into patient-centric risk and information-centric risks. Understanding the risk from these two perspectives can bring in a holistic strategic approach for health data management.

Assets Strategy

Organizations have assets both internal and external. Mainly, the health data which organizations are accountable to maintain is sprawled between organizational assets and third-party vendors. Health data analytics, health data storage, and interoperability are some of the major vendor services at present.

This will also bring in the challenge of how to determine assets' importance, risk, and impact. This solution lies heavily linked to information strategy. Managing assets not from system, team, or department's perspective but from information perspective is smart and sustainable. This will bring in clarity, accountability, and adaptability of assets based on sensitive information.

S—Sorting

By 2025, global estimates suggest 463 exabytes of data will be created each day. At present, the health data is increasing daily [7]. The interactions with digital health devices are estimated to increase by around 20-fold, which means that the digital health market is now a trillion-dollar market.

This innovation and usage of multiple devices creates a huge pool of data, and one of the big challenges healthcare has is how to sort the signal from the noise. Meaning, how can data of value be sorted from this huge pool of data?

The fifth industrial revolution has brought in the value of human and machine involvement in determining the innovation and technology needed. It has also brought in the concept of patient-driven healthcare.

At present, data sorting is performed at system-centric levels. This can bring in confusion and frustration in terms of its effectiveness and patient satisfaction. Data sorting performed with patient-centric level can bring in more visibility and high performance of data management.

Patient data-centric sorting will help to understand the patient data lifecycle through multiple systems, apps, and devices. It will also help to create a smart and sustainable ecosystem which can continuously perform with changes in technologies and integration.

Patient data-centric sorting also helps to create a patient profile faster which can help in providing high-quality treatments and health maintenance.

During pandemic, patient data-centric profiling from multiple systems, databases, and apps can help to:

- Understand the genetic profile
- Predict patient health

- Create a proactive information and response plan based on the symptoms
- Create global collaboration and customized response plan based on the patient's health profile

S—Synergy

Synergy is the big missing piece in the health industry at present. Synergy can mean different things for different organizations. Its meaning also differs from patient to providers and payers.

It is tempting to see and view synergy as purely technology based. But patient data-centric synergy will bring a sustainable and smart healthcare ecosystem.

The value of real-time patient data is now possible with the emerging tools and technology. The synergy between payers, providers, and patients can help create a strong and efficient healthcare ecosystem.

This synergy can be improved by creating a process in which:

- Patient profile can be created by leveraging technology, tools, and interoperability.
- Creating options of insurance, treatments, clinical trials, and other healthcare services.
- Maintaining and constantly evolving the options based on the real-time data.

Once the process is established, tools can help implement this process in a fast and efficient way.

Understanding the purpose and process before implementing a product in a process is the smart and strategic way to solve this bug in health data management puzzle.

CHAPTER 6

Implementing Strategic Data Management

Implementing the strategic health data management needs to start from the top.

The initial step is to develop strategic data governance and management policies. Data governance and management policies by the executives tend to be the working policy that centers around the management and administration of data resources and is a foundation of overseeing the undertaking of data resources. This policy ought to be overseen by a group inside the association that distinguishes how the policy is gotten to and utilized, who upholds the data, the executive's policy, and how it is conveyed to representatives.

In numerous associations, the chief information officer (CIO) and other senior administration can exhibit their comprehension of data significance to the executives by either writing or supporting orders that will be utilized to oversee and implement data norms.

There is a certain amount of argument on what policies are crucial data policy or digital policy. A digital policy which integrates data criticality, risk, impact, and innovation is smart and effective.

The following are a portion of the factors to consider in strategic data policies:

- Venture data isn't possessed by any individual or specialty unit; however, it is claimed by the undertaking.
- Endeavor data should be protected.
- Endeavor data must be accessible to appropriate people inside and outside the association.
- Metadata ought to be created and used for all organized and unstructured data.

- Data proprietors ought to be responsible for big business data.
- Clients ought to not stress over where data resides. Data ought to be available to clients regardless of where it dwells.
- Lastly, a data policy should direct your association's way of thinking toward overseeing data as an esteemed venture resource.

In terms of healthcare, these policies, too, are exponentially crucial as data and privacy cannot be breached, particularly owing to the strict data ownership and management laws that have been released under data ownership. These policies and big data, however, can also play a vital role in developing healthcare. One method, which has been quoted several times over the years, is Health in All Policies (Hip). According to the World Health Organization, the Hip is a method by which public policies across sectors systematically consider the health implications of decisions, seek synergies, and avoid harmful health impacts to improve population health and health equity.

As indicated by the global writing, the consequences of big data investigation should be helpful and significant to the two people and clinicians, so the maximum capacity of enormous data is utilized. Whenever dealt with effectively, big data can change healthcare, improve health results, and eventually shape lives. It can do this by conveying better caliber, more savvy healthcare. It can help reveal health determinants and propose proper consideration for people or populaces. Investigation of big data may empower revelations, influence results, diminish costs, and at the end of the day, better healthcare results. Analysts can utilize measurable models and apparatuses on big data to foresee danger or patterns and to help healthcare suppliers make strategies that improve results and are cost effective.

It is understood that AI, IoT, and ML help companies, and everyone involved get predictions on new data. These are the predictions that the healthcare sector and professionals can also use to make better use of data and strategic leadership.

All this data is up there. The challenge that arises for the leadership is to create a data strategy on data available, but the healthcare industry is one of the industries that remain highly regulated. These regulations tend to come in the way of using data through various means.

However, strategic data governance and management for the healthcare industry is essential. In all of this, the leadership is responsible for data governance, which remains the strategic approach to govern and manage data within the organization.

The next thing in line is the understanding of the organization's business model. It is crucial for organizations to understand their business model, especially if they generate some of the revenue from big data. Organizations whose products and services are based on big data can come under the following potential and upcoming markets:

- Patients' predictions for improved staffing
- Real-time alerting
- Electronic health records (EHRs)
- Enhancing patient engagement
- Prevent opioid abuse in the United States
- Predictive analytics in healthcare
- Reduce fraud and enhance security

Furthermore, understanding the business model will help create a strategic data management for enhancing customer experience, customer trust, and operational performance, among other things. The role of the leadership here is to consider all the above factors and create a format of governance that can bring in the customized data management designed specifically for the organization.

In totality, strategic data management for leadership needs to be looked at in a few different ways with varying considerations. It needs to have the initiative to change the organization's mindset or workforce to think about the factors and the true measure of success. In most cases, it would be data. This involves creating a roadmap for organizations which incorporates data criticality, risk, and impact. It also involves using multiple systems and processes mindfully to serve the patient better by understanding the patient and respecting their privacy at the same time.

More so, there is the need to create or update the processes required for improvement in data-centric effectiveness in terms of customer trust, operational performance, and public health improvement.

This strategic health data governance should create an environment of mindful innovation, ethical technology development, and safe sharing of patient data where privacy is not compromised. This can only be possible if privacy could be looked beyond systems and looked from a patient data-centric point of view.

CHAPTER 7

The Strategic Health Data Management Process

Times are changing. In the process of these changing times, one thing that has emerged phenomenally well has been data science. Data science is an integral part of data management.

Data Science at Strategic Use

Data science has triumphed at every peak that has ever existed in the world of business, science, and many other disciplines. Similarly, data science has been instrumental and has the potential to be even more instrumental in the future when it comes to healthcare.

One particularly integral part of data science is artificial intelligence. It has given the option of machine learning, and these two, when paired together, tend to become a recipe for revolution in the way that the healthcare sector operates in not just the United States but across the world. This, of course, has created new and better kinds of business opportunities in the same arena and made things a lot more efficient and a lot less prone to human error.

There could be several examples of this—one of these being medical imaging. Before the impact of data science, artificial intelligence, and machine learning on medical imaging is discussed, its prospect needs to be understood. Clinical pictures like computed tomography (CT), magnetic resonance imaging (MRI), mammograms, x-ray types like fluoroscopy and angiography, and ultrasounds are an important store of conceivably life-saving information for medical services specialists' suppliers and their patients.

In any case, these sorts of pictures likewise present exceptional difficulties that have generally restricted radiologists' viability in diagnosing and treating different afflictions. Consider that most clinical picture investigation today is performed by just a little bunch of (regularly exhausted) radiologists or clinical specialists. That implies the understanding of these sweeps is, best-case scenario, very abstract—and, even from a pessimistic standpoint, the sweeps can be altogether misguided.

Without a doubt, clinical specialists say one out of four patients experiences bogus positives from their clinical picture audit on account of such difficulties as commentator weakness and the expanding intricacy of the actual pictures. Moreover, keeping in mind that bogus positives are marginally better compared to bogus negatives—which can prompt a conceivably lethal condition going untreated—they're unquestionably awful, as they can prompt superfluous subsequent meet-ups or even a medical procedure.

Where all of this is well understood in terms of radiology particularly, it is also important to focus on the broader perspective of how digital science and the ability of digitalization can transform digital health. There are a few ways that this can be done. Let's look at a few options available as per experts.

Merging of Data Scientist and Physician

When the two positions are merged, the experience becomes unique. There is a post that is often referred to as chief data scientist that comes up, and the goal of this post is to look at various sources of data with the goal to improve patient outcomes. This includes data from a vast pool of information that comes from research data, clinical data, claims data, as well as the bills that are sent to the payers. Additionally, there are output sources too, which include reports on quality and more. Many questions and improvements can be investigated as one understands what drugs work for which patients, what are the differences between the results of trials and the results on actual patients, how many devices or medicines are needed for certain kinds of patients, and so many more things.

More so, this merger also makes the chief data scientist responsible for the organization of the concept of digital health itself. In the United States, prescriptions can be given out on applications on smartphones that are also FDA approved. This is one of the greater wins of digitalization in recent times of healthcare progression.

Data and Precision Medicine

It comes as no surprise that data is, in fact, the key to realizing the dream of precision medicine. The question comes up as to how data can be used and why it has become so important as it must achieve the overarching goal of precision medicine. This is because you cannot fall into precision medicine by just the measurements and the traditional way of looking at it. There need to be databases and tools allocated within artificial intelligence to know most of what is needed to be known. It is not only the most effective but also the safest and greatly cost-effective thing to do.

There are challenges to the situation as well. However, as of now, the prospects are brighter than any other aspect of digitization of healthcare and the involvement of databases along with artificial intelligence to make sense of things.

Patient-Defined Outcomes

When healthcare evolves, the most benefited group of people are the patients. Therefore, the outcomes must be patient oriented. For the outcomes to be patient oriented, the data collected should also be patient oriented. The concern, however, comes in when it is time to collect that data as many why's and how's tower upon the researchers—there must be a way out.

The solution to that is seen in the idea that either information is outrightly acquired or the healthcare professionals need to do a better job at understanding their patients. This includes all the intricacies from the time that they came into the system to the time that they leave the system.

Where that is one and a rather simple way to take care of this, there are better ways that need to be adopted by people the world over. There needs to be a change in the cultural mindset to get the patients to share their data and health systems to use more patient-reported data to drive clinical decisions.

Data Usage

There are many prospects and many more solutions for the concern. There are also a few recommendations that might come in handy when looking at data usage in healthcare transformation and value-based care.

Regard Your Data

Healthcare Data Management (HDM) without aligning vision and the goal in terms of patient care is like travelling without a roadmap. It is expensive and ineffective. Modern healthcare is bombarded with the data from IoT devices, hospital systems, and proactive usage of digital health apps. This massive collection of data without a proper definition and direction of use toward patient care is expensive and unproductive. Also, not considering the patient data sensitive information security and privacy in HDM is dangerous as it can lead to data breaches. Comprehend that patient information is delicate; it must be secured as it's coming from patients. Regarding the data in terms of the following points can help build strategic and lean health data management:

- Alignment with the critical need of patient care.
- Alignment with sensitive patient information privacy and security.
- Alignment with treatment of data with patient trust, fairness, and empathy as the core measure of success.
- Consistent efforts of safeguard and guarantee of data utilization in alignment with patient trust.

Utilize Your Data

Present era of abundant digital technologies and overwhelming acceptability of using them leads to humungous data availability. This is also true in the healthcare industry. Besides the challenges on how to manage this big data, the billion-dollar question is how to utilize it to enhance patient care and services. Most of the healthcare organizations at present struggle with the overwhelming and siloed patient records which contain both personal and health information from various data sources from diagnostics, clinical trial platforms, IoT, and other healthcare systems. Data utilization choices need to be one of the key focus points for organization's success. Organizations probably won't remember that they have that data. Thus, understanding the data, the list of data, the stock of data organizations have, and how to utilize it will be increasingly significant.

Innovate With Your Data

Future advancements in medical services are, and will be data driven. From clinical records on cell phones to telemedicine records, there is abundance of data with technologies playing critical role in creating them, it only makes sense to ask, are we using it to its full potential to enhance patient care? The data coming from CAT checks, clinical trials, and Internet of Medical Things (IoMT) could really help to create a proactive or customized healthcare for patients. So, innovating with data is a basic need now. It needs a deep understanding of organizations' vision and mission toward patient care. The data with innovation in mind needs to be consciously enhanced in a safe and secure way.

At present, there is a certain amount of clarity over the immense potential of data through data science, artificial intelligence, and data statistics.

Resources

There is a critical need of data ownership and hiring sharp data owners. This ownership will smoothen the process and make things much easier. These roles will bring in a holistic view of data management from multiple angles of management, leadership, customer trust, and overall patient care effectiveness.

Unique Roles of Small Organizations

Just like any business, smaller healthcare organizations play just as big a part as the bigger healthcare organizations towards patient care. The sensitive patient data collection is mostly similar among these organizations.

For all these things to happen, there are a multitude of goals that are set to make things happen. After these goals, there is the need to create strategic efficiency through these strategic goals, particularly in terms of data. Such goals include overcoming the regulatory challenge, which is the security of data, and the assertion of ISO in security officers. These are the goals that strongly push forward the prospects of data in healthcare.

Attentive Investments

Hans Keil explains that healthcare investment is the key to success, and this includes not just data management but also talent, techniques, and technology all working together in a certain kind and sort of harmony. When one talks about strategic data management, what they are truly referring to is the identification of data of value. Now, the next thing to clarify is how data is valued. More so, when one talks about identifying the value of data, they are specifically talking about systems, marketing, clinical outcomes, revenue, and supply chain.

One of the biggest challenges, however, in this process of valuation and digitalization comes in the form of data duplication. When there is a plethora of unending information to tackle, chances are there might be duplication. For example, the same patient could be in the category of diabetics while also being in the category of heart patients, which might just make data regarding the patient being confused, especially if coming from different sources. There isn't much as of now to counter that challenge. However, this can be controlled to a certain extent by narrowing down the critical sources of data.

Once this challenge has been effectively overcome, the value of data is what becomes the prime focus again. This is the understanding that data intersection is extremely crucial to avoid nonprofit friction and more. What happens is that as soon as this gets into a working flow, the cycle begins to feed on each other. One after the other, things begin happening in a domino effect where they become dependent on each other as well. It becomes about big needle movers, significant service, and an increase in profitability.

In all of this, one thing that needs to be kept in mind is that interoperability of data utilization will bring in better outcomes overall.

A list of experts was interviewed for this book. Albert is a social entrepreneur looking to change how healthcare examines health data and what global impact this data can have. The few decades of him being in the health industry have brought up an irreplaceable and deep view of the present health data management view. It is due to people like him that in the healthcare ecosystem, there is a sense of health data ownership by organizations. This, of course, includes all data as well as the patient's particular data.

Another expert to be taken seriously here must be Matthew Taylor, who is a vice president in solutions at a large health IT organization, where his specialty lies in population health and health IT. He has vast, intriguing experience in multiple healthcare organizations. He talks about patient-centric healthcare too. Health IT is seeing a new wave of needs, which certainly include personalized patient healthcare. Let us dwell deeper into this idea before breaking down into what Taylor has to say.

This wave is something that the world has overtaken. The solutions that come need to be from the perspective of the patient and the loved ones of that very patient. Every specimen to be processed needs to have a patient associated with it, and healthcare organizations must not lose sight of that idea. The systems that are being managed across need to be developed to focus fundamentally on improving the existing service. One of the biggest contributors to the cause can be artificial intelligence, and a brilliant application platform can come with the use of telehealth.

Now, back to what Taylor has to say about the situation. He argues that there are four big challenges present in healthcare now, particularly regarding data and data management.

He believes that the quantity of the data is increasing by the second. This is due to the massive influx through medical device providers that include health applications and diagnostics. When the quantity increases, it becomes difficult to manage, and when the management becomes a problem, duplication begins to happen.

This duplication then leads to incorrect data, which in a way kills the entire point of the whole process. This also brings a challenge of parsing quality data from this high data quantity. He spoke:

The challenge we have now is to separate signals from the noise.

Signal Versus Noise

In this vast pool of inevitable data created and collected by healthcare organizations, the challenge healthcare has is how to pull out the *data* of value from this pool. This value of data may be defined differently by different organizations.

Data Privacy

Where there is so much data being gathered around the world for healthcare, the question of privacy is inevitable. With all the information present, it becomes an absolute debacle to decide and then also determine what data remains restricted and what needs to be restricted. It is a dilemma that hits many researchers and information collectors worldwide, making it a challenge worth tackling.

Data Ownership

As mentioned earlier, there is plenty of data out there. The more data there is, the more stakeholders will come into the picture. When more people are involved, there comes the question of ownership. There are technological partnerships, patients, healthcare providers, present integrated systems along with business partnerships involved in the process. The decision as to who owns the data tends to become problematic. This, in turn, creates problems for the process to function properly.

Interoperability

This as a challenge is rather self-explanatory. Where the dependence of all the aspects on one another can be beneficial, it can also become a challenge. This is the case because the lack of functionality on one aspect can cause damage to the entire cycle, and before one knows it, the cycle would not be functional anymore. Independent aspects tend to also be rather useless without their counterparts.

These are the challenges that were put forth by experts, and many other experts will probably agree with all of these. What one needs to understand and truly comprehend is the idea and fact, rather, that even though digitalization has begun within the healthcare realms and the systems that take care of the healthcare systems, it still hasn't been flawlessly implemented and this implementation could take some time. Furthermore, this implementation also brings us to an important aspect: data collection and the challenges surrounding it.

CHAPTER 8

Best Health Data Management Practices

Health data management process starts from data creation and collection to its retrieval and archival. This chapter describes strategies related to parts of data management process—data collection and data analytics.

At present, the missing piece in HDM is defining the data needs before data collection stage. The initial and crucial step of data management is to define:

- The data sets that need to be collected
- The requirements of data types
- The data sources from which data sets need to be collected.

Data collection is one of the first crucial steps which need strategy. Strategic data collection can save millions of dollars and can save months and years of time.

Data Collection

Throughout the entire HDM process, health data collection is not often discussed, which is one of the biggest mistakes. It is one of the first and the most crucial step which needs to be keenly observed, assessed, and examined. Data collection remains particularly challenging for hospitals, because hospitals, on their own, are a chaotic system, to begin with. There are emergencies all around, so when there is data coming from 13 or 14 different systems overall, there is an increase in confusion when it comes to assessing and standardizing the data.

All these different systems have different formats of data, too, because data collection is happening with different systems and in different data formats. This increases the workload on those working to gather the data, and if the data is being gathered automatically through machines, then the machines, too, can be filtered with.

This is critical in the process and must be taken into consideration. There are many other challenges of data being collected which include, but are not limited to the following:

- Different data standards or formats on different systems
- Different data sets from different systems
- Unharmonized data
- Unclear data priority and impact

The next step is to describe the roadmap on how things can be done. The first question to answer here is how to strategize the data collection and why it is as essential as it is? Here is why.

There has been more data produced over the most recent two years than during the entire of humankind's set of experiences. It should be prepared, put away, and dissected for use. That is the reason for data assortment. It intends to explore a specific theme or territory and investigate it for settling on the right choices. Refreshed and precise data can fundamentally improve the outcomes, regardless of whether utilized for individual, public, or legislative issues.

Nonetheless, current advances at this point don't adapt to tremendous volumes of data, prompting terrible showing, lost incomes, and sitting around. As indicated by Forbes, 95 percent of organizations have issues overseeing data and are searching for a compelling arrangement.

Medical care is a powerful industry that executes the most recent innovations and instruments to track and dissect data about patients, clinics, and other clinical frameworks. Data assortment apparatuses help get a clearer image of a patient's well-being, oversee data rapidly, and share it with different experts inside a solitary snap.

Powerful assortment and the executives of data can be a key to the commitment of patients and their treatment. That is the reason why recruiting medical care programming engineers and getting a redone answer for a business might perhaps be the best choice.

Now, how can these be collected? Some of these might be repetitions from the previous chapters; however, it is crucial to put focus on these ideas to ensure their implementation in the best possible way. It is likely and quite possibly the most successive inquiries that specialists and organizations pose when choosing to assemble and store data effectively. Luckily, numerous devices help assess projects, connect assessments and conventions, and cooperate with center gatherings.

The first and most urgent advance is to pick a technique that suits organization's specific venture's requirements and objectives. Here are a few inquiries that may help:

- What data needs to be gathered?
- Why is it important?
- How directly it impacts the patient?

Right now, the healthcare business is changing to a computerized space rather than meetings and papers. Here are the most well-known strategies for gathering data in healthcare:

- **Customer relationship management (CRM)**
  These frameworks permit gathering and taking care of data from different directs and putting them away in one spot. They likewise break down data and are safely put away inside an organization. There are operational, key, insightful, and community CRMs focused on explicit objectives.

- **Electronic health record (EHR)**
  EHR innovation is like CRM. It assists with gathering and dissecting data and sharing it across clinics and different foundations. EHRs can incorporate such data as clinical history, hypersensitivities, inoculation, radiology pictures, and individual measurements. More than 94 percent of U.S.-based emergency clinics and over 60 percent of private clinical suppliers are now utilizing EHR frameworks.

- **Portable applications**

  Applications that suddenly spike in demand for cell phones and tablets can interface patients and medical clinics, assemble data, and store it in databases. They establish a quick and secure climate between a specialist and a patient and fundamentally save time.

Right now, the market leans toward business programming, yet the advantages of custom items are obvious. These instruments are customized to a specific foundation's requirements and may essentially improve the administrations' quality. To track down the most ideal choice, clinical associations ought to think about their administrations, the number of patients and attendants, their financial plan, and foundation.

With that, let us tap into data inputs and what they really are. The thing is that each system has different data inputs and understanding these will help to understand the crucial impact it tends to have. When a device is configured through a task, the values that are to be set to the attributes must be supplied to the task before it gets executed. In the case of the task being template-based, these data will form as inputs to the parameterized placeholders of the template, which includes inventory input, network element input, and user inputs. Once you know these, you need to understand the data standard for all the systems involved.

Strategic Data Analytics

An integral step into understanding data science is data analytics. Data analytics is the study of examining crude data to make decisions about that data. Many strategies and cycles of data analytics have been computerized into mechanical cycles and calculations that work over crude data for human utilization.

Data analytics methods can uncover patterns and measurements that would somehow or other be lost in the mass of data. This data would then be able to be utilized to upgrade cycles to expand the general effectiveness of a business or framework. Let us understand it better.

Data analytics is an expansive term that includes numerous assorted sorts of data investigation. Any kind of data can be exposed to data analytics methods to get the knowledge that can be utilized to improve things.

For instance, fabricating organizations frequently record the runtime, vacation, and work line for different machines and afterward investigate the data to more likely arrange the jobs, so the machines work nearer to the top limit.

Data analytics can do substantially more than call attention to bottlenecks underway. Gaming organizations use data analytics to set prize timetables for players that keep most of the players dynamic in the game. Content organizations utilize a considerable lot of similar data analytics to keep you clicking, watching, or re-sorting out substance to get another view or another snap.

The interaction engaged with data investigation includes a few distinct advances:

- The initial step is to decide the data prerequisites or how the data is assembled. Data might be isolated by age, segment, pay, or sex. Data might be mathematical or be isolated by class.
- The second step in data analytics is the way toward gathering it. This should be possible through an assortment of sources like PCs, online sources, cameras, ecological sources, or staff.
- When the data is gathered, it should be coordinated, so it tends to be examined. Association may happen on a bookkeeping page or other type of programming that can take measurable data.
- The data is then tidied up before examination. This implies it is scoured and checked to guarantee there is no duplication or mistake and that it isn't fragmented. This progression rectifies any mistakes before it goes on to a data examiner to be investigated.

Basically, data analytics could be defined as the study of dissecting crude data to make decisions about that data. Moreover, the procedures and cycles of data analytics have been robotized into mechanical cycles and calculations that work over crude data for human utilization. Data analytics assists a business with streamlining its presentation as well, and these are just some of the things that are involved in the process. Next, let us look at why it matters.

Data analytics is significant because it assists organizations with streamlining their exhibitions. Executing it into the plan of action implies that organizations can help decrease costs by recognizing more productive methods of working together and putting away a lot of data. An organization can likewise utilize data analytics to settle on better business choices and help examine client patterns and fulfillment, which can prompt new—and better—items and administrations.

Now comes the real question. Who is using data analytics, and how far is the medical industry into making use of it? In fact, a portion of the areas that have embraced the utilization of data analytics incorporate the movement and cordiality industry, where turnarounds can be snappy. This industry can gather client data, sort out where the issues are, assume any untruth, and fix them.

Medical services join the utilization of high volumes of organized and unstructured data and utilization data analytics to settle on snappy choices. Also, the retail business utilizes overflowing measures of data to fulfill the constantly changing needs of customers. The data that retailers gather and break down can assist them with recognizing patterns, suggest items, and increment benefits.

It wouldn't be an incorrect assumption to make if one put forth the argument that data analytics is a crucial part of the present healthcare industry. The health industry is at present divided into three categories:

- Patients
- Payers
- Providers

All three of these tend to use data analytics to the best of their use and make healthcare as efficient as possible, particularly regarding healthcare management. This can be a safe assumption to make because data analytics businesses are at an all-time high and can transform any healthcare business to its invincible and highly profitable status. Different kinds of analytics are discussed on a more general level.

In the healthcare industry, there are a few kinds of analytics:

- Descriptive analytics
- Predictive analytics
- Prescriptive analytics
- Diagnostic analytics

There are no two ways about the fact that data analytics need to be standardized, and a set of robust processes need to be implemented. Some big hospitals are even going further and using EHR data analytics to improve and aggressively transform reporting and outcomes. Moreover, physicians and frontline workers are challenged with data analytics outcomes and how to understand and serve the patient better. As a result, hospital data analytics now contains data from multiple patient-related systems like health applications, medical devices, and other unstandardized ways and devices for the same.

There are, of course, ways how data analytics can be strategized. There are no concrete solutions, but ones that tend to come with trial and error, but with caution. First and foremost, one can create a prioritized set of data coming from systems and applications, and this can be done based on factors like patient impact, revenue impact, and quality service impact. Other ways could include the likes of organization of data into categories. This way might require a certain amount of labor in the beginning, but, in the long run, it will help the cause.

In all of this, what remains constant is the importance of data and how it is managed. If the data is managed well, through the many ways discussed in the chapter, the efficiency of the healthcare system in a digitalized system is likely to be close to a hundred percent. Data is important, and so is data management, and where healthcare might be just one of the many industries impacted by this revolution of data, it is still an integral part of the data and digital revolution.

CHAPTER 9

Strategic Health Data Management During Pandemics

In the present world, it is almost impossible to talk about healthcare without talking about how particular aspects of healthcare respond to pandemics or what the scope of all that remains. In short, the question comes down to how strategic data management can help avoid and control pandemics. The thing is that pandemics like COVID-19 tend to challenge the overall global pandemic planning and operations.

Over the course of the COVID pandemic, healthcare operators around the globe have been required to rapidly deploy new tools and technologies at an unprecedented pace, and for any given project, the integration of multiple (and often sensitive) data sources may be required:

- Supply chain/inventory data
- Public health data/EHR
- Legacy system data
- Contact tracing data
- Vaccination data
- Geographic/hotspot data
- SaaS app data
- AI/ML data

In the case of health pandemics, it is crucial to keep a few things in mind.

- Understand what the critical health data sets are.
- Understand the health data sets' origin—geolocation.

- Analyze the healthcare data attributes for predictive and decisive outcomes. This includes cure as well as future planning.

Once these pointers are taken into consideration, one also needs to be mindful of the fact that strategic data management during pandemics like COVID-19 should include a collaborative approach from multiple countries, states, and even counties. One great example of that could be the invention as well as the distribution of the COVID-19 vaccine. The pandemic might have seen a sense of closure with the vaccine without a lot of strategic development on data globally, but when it came to the cure, many countries joined hands to create a solution. This shows the value and impact of collaboration.

Effective Data Operations Through Data Centricity

An interview with Dan Demers, entrepreneur and senior IT executive, and Chris McLellan, founder of Askai.org, unleashes the current progress in HDM operations. Data Fabric architecture and Dataware-based solutions are eliminating traditional data integration and helping healthcare service providers to accelerate IT delivery while improving data protection and data governance.

Data control through access not making copies is one of the best solutions, for example, giving patients access to all the data from medical devices, and application in one centralized location rather than duplication.

There is a continuous ever-growing technology and complexity. Each organization is going through growing complexity due to implementing technology, but innovation cannot simplify but rather make a process complex; it will eventually choke innovation. As healthcare tangles through more technology, application, and integration, it will either reverse or collapse.

The point to be made here is that once the strategy of the health data management plan is determined, then the next step should be to find the tools and platform which are able to execute the plan that has just been created after much deliberation.

CHAPTER 10

Myths and Reality About Pandemic Health Data Management

This chapter contains the basic myths or assumptions of pandemic health data management.

Myth 1: Only Technology Can Solve This Problem

This is a rather bold assumption to make. The *reality* of the matter is that strategic planning and processing come before technology does in this regard. Of course, technology and tools are a huge part of the process, but they come after roadmap is planned, and the plans need to be executed. It is basically the execution of the plans and processes that require technology, not the plan itself. The tools and technology can help to provide predictive analysis to create a roadmap and it is not the roadmap itself. Ultimately, the roadmap is created with the combination of information obtained from tools and technology and strategies created with empathy and vision for better future.

Myth 2: It Is Easy to Standardize Data That Helps Implement Pandemic Response Quickly

Data standardization on its own is one of the biggest challenges in the present healthcare system, where there are different systems, locations, and ecosystems that have differing health data standards. This has become a big challenge when a collaborative effort needs to come into place, and there is a huge prospect for this to become an organization as a global alliance and global effort by everyone involved.

As more technology and tools are included, it is very important to understand what data standards are adopted by these individual technologies or tools. Visibility and synergizing data formats are the crucial process. This can bring in effectiveness and highly performing pandemic health data management.

Myth 3: Agnostic and Comprehensive Data Is Merely a Need

COVID has shown that science is changing constantly, and rapidly as new side effects are revealed and with the latest variety of sickness. To really comprehend what's going on, there is a need of data that communicates in a typical language or that can be deciphered through man-made consciousness or AI to be translatable.

There is the need at this point to have subject matter experts (SMEs) set up who comprehend the data and can guarantee the data that is accessible is right for the calculations to be run.

It is crucial to understand the present and future pandemic HDM challenges and possible strategic solutions to improve by strategic use of agnostic and comprehensive data.

Myth 4: Global View Is Not Necessary

Part of the test with COVID, and conceivably with future general well-being crises, has been the public communication. The test of that normal reaction is one that should be smoothed out and conveyed early and frequently to abstain from misconception.

There additionally should be a clear correspondence between federal organizations and states as for reaction and capacities. The Centers for Disease Control and Prevention saw its labs overpowered by the sheer quantities of tests required and needed to go to private and different labs to deal with the heap.

As the myths tend to get clarified, it is important to understand that data, mapping a data strategy, and effectively implementing strategic data management. Artificial intelligence and other technologies have a huge role to play in predictive, strategic health management and disaster recovery analytics.

Myth 5: Present Clinical Trials Landscape Is Efficient

Clinical trials are the most critical phase for pharma. It requires the collaboration between many stakeholders, such as researchers, administrators, clinical trials patients, hospitals, and hospital staff. Clinical data continually changes, as do the names, callings, areas, and states of patients and doctors. Patients go through various tests and are directed to numerous sorts of treatment throughout the long term, and the medicines and prescriptions themselves develop over the long haul. New kinds of clinical treatment, for example, telehealth models, make new sorts of data.

Clinical trials management has begun to greatly transform over recent years and has been hastened by the pandemic. Clinical trials management is increasingly digitized, and this digitalization is continuously transforming the efficiency and performance of clinical trials.

Clinical data management is a key component, and this pandemic has proven its importance more than ever. Present clinical trial landscape is transforming at a faster rate with inclusion of digitalization. It has also brought in the challenges of data management.

But there are still a lot of challenges to address. An interview with Adam Samson unleashes the challenges and possible ways to address them.

Diversity and Inclusion

Clinical trials management is a key aspect of drug development. A high and diverse quality of data sets can bring in effective and safe vaccines or drugs to the market.

At present, the diversity of population is a big challenge. Some might include the following:

- Access to clinical trials can be hard for some communities because of commute issues, trying to find the time in working days for follow-ups.
- Distrust in the clinical trials process. Awareness on the quality and integrity of clinical trials processes need to be communicated to the communities to build and improve trust on clinical trial operations.

Interoperability Role in Clinical Trials

At present, many of those working in clinical trials have limited access to real-time clinical data. Having a centralized and common data system which is accessible to participants, doctors, investigators, and clinical researchers involved in clinical trials is the key for success.

Clinical trial participants, doctors, investigators, and clinical researchers need real-time appropriate data during the entire clinical trial process. Silo systems and data in them used by all these key players are impacting the effectiveness and collaboration.

Interoperability plays a major role and can bring in the visibility of real-time data to all these clinical trial teams.

This will further bring in the highest collaboration between multiple systems used by multiple clinical trials team members ranging from doctors, clinicians, to patients.

In conclusion, pandemic healthcare management exposed the present vulnerabilities in health data management. It also provided a path forward to build an effective and secure patient data-centric healthcare system learning from these vulnerabilities. This efficient system could be built by understanding patient data and with an undeniable continuous effort to build patient trust. Patient trust could be built by implementing and continuously monitoring appropriate risk-based privacy and security controls.

CHAPTER 11

Global Strategic Health Data Management

One rather important concern throughout healthcare data management (HDM), especially when it comes to working strategically through data on a global level, comes from the concern of data protectionism. The term data protectionism is a famous and global term that is often used by businesses globally as well as locally.

Tremendous measures of data are traded across the world nowadays, yet its progression is restricted by countries putting limitations on where it very well may be gathered and how it can be managed.

This is the extremely old issue of exchange protectionism warmed for the advanced age. Be that as it may, there is likewise an additional turn brought about by the characteristic social and individual nature of most data. It very well may be managed by building a data foundation that ensures security while boosting advancement.

Numerous regulations and standards like HIPAA, GDPR, and ISO27701 are established to provide governance and guidance around privacy and security of personal identifiable and health information.

Other contributing components incorporate things like data sets, principles, innovation, direction, and the associations that steward data. Research proposes that getting those pieces set up and building a solid data foundation that is as open as possible increment the trust that residents have in data assortment, sharing, and use, and that there is a risk in not doing as such.

Global data flows can bring an invaluable and possible global impact and progress, but personal and health data privacy is a big concern.

In an interview with Gil Bashe, he mentioned that health data protectionism is one of the big challenges healthcare has at present. This protectionism is from hospitals and other health organizations.

There are several reasons for protectionism in the health industry, including competitive advantage, business advantage, and consumer/patient advantage. He quoted:

> We need to find ways where we can share the health data without compromising security and privacy. This sharing and collaboration will open new ways to create a stronger and smarter health ecosystem.

It is increasingly becoming important for data to be shared globally for the sake of a better and efficient health system through the best data management systems and processes; there is also a need to understand and find new ways to securely share health data.

For this purpose, Dan Weaver, helps us understand things a little better, along with a few ways that the process can be made easier.

In an interview with Dan Weaver, he explains that health data protectionism is one of the big challenges healthcare has at present. This protectionism is from hospitals and other health organizations.

There are several reasons for protectionism in the health industry, including competitive advantage, business advantage, and consumer/patient advantage.

> We need to find ways where we can share the health data without compromising security and privacy. This sharing and collaboration will open new ways to create a stronger and smarter health ecosystem. One of the current ways is by removing Personal identifiers from Personal health information data.

He elaborates it further by saying that we need to improve the irreversibility of de-identification methods to protect an anomaly and we need to devise innovative new techniques for sharing health data that further secures patients' interest.

He describes this will help us to create a huge amount of data sets and safely share them with innovative communities.

Accelerate Innovation

As healthcare associations embrace more worth-based care conveyance models, the joining of data and data resources into care conveyance will be table stakes. Healthcare suppliers should have the option to use their one-of-a-kind situation as makers and aggregators of data to improve the patient experience and results and decrease cost.

Tailoring Inherent Permission and Consent Into Product Design

Permission and consent reinforced by the legal system will build trust by patients in sharing their data and benefiting commensurately, thus encouraging appropriate data sharing by patients. In other words, because the patient can trust in the legal system to assist them in controlling and benefitting from their data, they will begin to broker it voluntarily, given agreeable terms of protection/privacy/compensation/and so on. Incorporating the key principles of respecting the individual and their rights will build a strong trust relationship with the patient. Some of the forms this can implemented is by proactive permission and consent before data sharing.

CHAPTER 12

Strategic Data Management for the Future

Building trust between the patient, providers, and payers is mandatory. Data ownership and access to patient data are very crucial and need to be understood carefully. Data should be literally owned by the individual to whom it applies. With ownership and property rights come control. The patients will legally control the existence and use of their data. Any use of data in this context will require the explicit permission of the owner/patient and can be controlled by the patient for various cases (e.g., exclusion/prohibition, partial access, full access, temporary/transient access, permanent access, sharing, leasing, sale, donation).

Creating such an ecosystem based on the principle of "Respect the individual; respect individual rights" can bring in a strong and secure trust relationship.

As the technology emerges and transforms healthcare at a faster rate, the regulators are challenged to create laws, standards, and regulations which can help guide the innovation.

National and state laws could be modified to confer property rights to the individual over their own data, so common law practices regarding privately owned property can begin to be leveraged regarding data rights. (A good analogy is the land/real-estate markets that have arisen now as clear title and protection can be gained over land.)

Graphing the Change

It can be said that the COVID-19 pandemic has changed the world. In generic terms, it has changed the world for the worse, where economic, social, and cultural aspects may find themselves ruptured. However, as far as medicine and data management are concerned, the COVID-19 pandemic has opened a bleak window of opportunity to allow nations to come together and investigate making a global impact through data sharing, management, and then application of that management. The world cannot take another pandemic if it were to come any time soon, with the kind of healthcare structure that stands around most of the world.

It is advised to take upon the opportunity and plan better data management strategies to ensure that the healthcare sectors across the globe take full advantage of digitalization, artificial intelligence, machine learning, and all the other aspects that come as part and parcel of a global healthcare plan—all of this keeping data protectionism in mind. The emergency will disappear, yet the longing for a superior, more effective healthcare framework—one where unmistakably the data can do a great deal of use for a ton of major parts in all aspects of the ecosystem—will remain.

These are just some observations of how artificial intelligence has played its vital part in ensuring that the pandemic has been taken care of in at least as many ways as possible. More so, the acceleration in global health cooperation is no surprise to anyone as it came as an inevitable step. This has paved the way for more cooperation to happen globally to ensure a transition into healthcare cooperation, particularly with secure data, without the pandemic situation as well.

Create High-Quality Healthcare

This one remains rather self-explanatory. The more strategic the data management is, and the more the world shares with one another for research and its implementation, the better the healthcare system will find itself in. Better research means better implementation, and better implementation, of course, means quality healthcare services for the patients, as well as the healthcare providers and their ease.

Accelerate High Quality and Implementation of Tech Like AI and ML

Countries across the globe are considering AI and ML as primary healthcare forms and measures. However, there might be some nations around the world that struggle with the implementation, especially when compared with medically advanced nations like Israel and Singapore. In that regard, a global cooperation and sharing of data and its strategic management from both ends are going to accelerate the high quality and implementation of the platforms, again making healthcare more efficient and accessible. At the end of the day, what matters is better healthcare, and that is a solution and situation that the acceleration of artificial intelligence and machine learning provides. Strategic healthcare data management (SHDM) is a compilation of strategies adapted for better and smart healthcare for patients and process of leveraging the value of technologies implementing these strategies.

Create Smart and Personalized Healthcare Ecosystem

This one has the most amount of information that needs to be grasped. Ecosystems make amazing powers that can reshape and upset industries. In healthcare, they can possibly convey a customized and incorporated insight to patients, upgrade supplier profitability, and improve results and affordability. Ecosystem can be defined as a bunch of capacities and administrations that coordinate with chain members (clients, providers, and stage and specialist organizations) through a typical business model and virtual data spine (empowered via consistent data catch, management, and trade) to make improved and proficient patient care.

Healthcare has moved away from its post-World War II spotlight on infectious sickness and work environment mishaps, which required roundabout interventions. Today, the essential objective is forestalling and adequately overseeing constant conditions. Nonetheless, as it appears, profitability in healthcare is slacking different administration ventures as these objectives shift. New innovations guarantee care that is accessible close by or at home, upholds ceaseless self and self-ruling consideration, and lessens grinding costs between supporting partners. One might think what an efficient ecosystem could be capable of; well here are just some of the advantages of it:

- Address industry shortcomings regularly by advancing underutilized resources/assets or wiping out grinding in patient experience.

- Advantage from network impacts, because as they develop, they make more incentive for providers (for instance, gig drivers or application designers) and patients the same.
- Own something in scant inventory that gives vital influence on the ecosystem administrator.
- Utilize the data produced in the ecosystem (for instance, buy examples or review practices) to tailor answers for providers and patients.

The healthcare ecosystems of things to come, as different ecosystems, will be fixated on the buyer, for this situation, the patient. The abilities and administrations that structure the healthcare ecosystems of things to come will incorporate, yet are not restricted to:

- Custom consideration: direct consideration and drugs controlled by suppliers, across conventional destinations of care.
- Customized home and self-care: patient commitment, self- and virtual consideration, far-off observing, and customary consideration that can progressively be conveyed close by or in the home.
- Social consideration: social and local area networks identified with a patient's all-encompassing health zeroed in on local area components of neglected social requirements.
- Day-by-day life exercises: patient activities and propensities empowering well-being and health, including wellness and sustenance.
- Financing support: tasks and monetary foundation supporting industry care occasions, including installment and financing arrangements.

Every one of these abilities and administrations adds to the fundamental data spine and progress examination innovations. These abilities keep up data respectability and empower bits of knowledge from the ecosystem.

Integrate Patients' Data Rights Management in Healthcare Ecosystem

Present healthcare ecosystem has ever-changing technologies (like IoT), tools, and platforms where patient data is sprawled. This includes but is not limited to IoT, digital health applications, health data management platforms, and more. This leads to major challenges on patient's data rights' clarity on:

- Patient's data location
- Patient's data access
- Patient's data collection
- Patient's data sharing
- Patient's data processing, storage, and more

It is critical and invaluable to integrate the patients' data rights management (PDRM) in the healthcare ecosystem. This will help to comply with privacy regulations and standards. This also brings the roadmap on the accountability of organization, suppliers, and patients throughout the healthcare data lifecycle and in turn helps to create effective healthcare ecosystem.

Perform Strategic Analysis Impacting Patient's Trust and Healthcare Business

HDM is based on three factors:

- Patient's data of value
- Effort to build and maintain patient's trust
- Improve impact and effectiveness of healthcare for patients

The above factors must be considered and analyzed in the process of creating effective HDM. Building these factors in the HDM infrastructure will bring business advantage and competitive advantage.

In conclusion, it is important to create a smart and personalized patient healthcare ecosystem where the data spine from multiple sources like medical devices, apps, and hospitals is completely used to its full potential. This can be possible by implementing a strategic digitized approach on healthcare data.

CHAPTER 13

Path to the Future

Numerous interviews were conducted as part of the research for this book. Below is a compilation of messages from the interviews.

Message From Leaders to Leaders

It is not always about the tools and technology; it is mostly about the process. Leaders interviewed for this book concur that a roadmap for organizations need to be created with a vision of strategic healthcare data management. The technology needs to be assessed properly and placed at appropriate stages of process to take advantage of its full potential. Placing the tools without understanding their role in the big picture will bring in more challenges like data silos, unclarity, and more operational cost for organizations.

Message to Healthcare Professionals

Do not underestimate the power of technology. The efficiencies we can gain with technology, pairing the operational skills, patient-centric approach, and technology can lead to efficient and high-quality healthcare. For example, pairing the clinical operational skills with technology can lead to efficient and high-quality clinical trials.

Message to Academia

A collaborative effort with administration is needed to help understand the changes in the need for adaptable and centralized health data.

Message to Entrepreneurs

Strategic health data management is a billion-dollar market yet to be explored. It will not only reduce operational cost and time for many organizations, but also bring in the health data of value in the right place at the right time. Innovation with intellect can help build a smart health ecosystem where effective digitalized patient care is at the center.

CHAPTER 14

Conclusion

All that needed to be discussed in the book has already been done. However, to wrap things up, it would make sense to bring it all together as a summary and see where healthcare and data management stand today with one another to make lives better.

Health information is progressively digitized, and, as in most different businesses, information is filling in velocity, volume, and value. Healthcare Data Management (HDM) is the act of sorting out this information and overseeing it to the advantage of medical services associations, experts, and eventually persistent prosperity and well-being. "Strategic healthcare data management is a common way to communicate, collaborate, and connect between clients and organizations"

Peruse on to realize what sorts of information are overseen in HDM, the advantages, and interesting difficulties of the field, including high information volume, its security contemplations, its risk, use, impact, and measures to stay away from information privacy while putting away medical services information.

As health data management advances with more inclusion of personalization and technology, more associations will gather a bigger assortment of health-related data and incorporate it to produce new experiences that can upgrade patient health.

In this process, it is also important to look at the benefits of strategic health data management.

- Highly personalized health data can help to create a high-quality precision medicine.
- Make a complete patient profiling with key data elements from multiple sources.
- Improve patient commitment and satisfaction.

- Improve health results—track health patterns in specific zones or among explicit populaces, foresee new patterns, and propose proactive measures to counter rising health issues.
- Business dynamic—help healthcare suppliers settle on better data-driven choices, for example, which kinds of clinical experts to enlist, what gear to put resources into, or which sorts of patients to zero in on in advertising endeavors.
- Integrated ethical approach—help define and implement the ethical and intellect parameters of healthcare using technology.

Here are a couple of significant challenges strategic data management could solve. Some include:

- Reengineering siloed data
- Parsing quality data from huge data pool
- Management of the data of value for patients and organization
- Saving operational cost and time
- Innovation with intellect
- Creating highly personalized and effective patient service

Modern times, particularly the COVID-19 pandemic, have exposed the vulnerabilities and loopholes of the present healthcare system and the way this data has been managed. There are better and more efficient ways that need to be utilized to ensure that medical histories, global pandemic real data, as well as medical research are not compromised in the process of being fast-paced and, in some cases, being simply inefficient.

As one example, if one were to take a COVID patient and not manage their data correctly, there are going to be so many things at risk. For starters, the patient's medical history is at risk of being lost, which means that they cannot be guaranteed post-COVID care in the best possible way that they deserve. Similarly, losing patient's COVID-related data will hinder research into information about the virus, which would eventually lead to inefficient vaccination opportunities and better tackling techniques.

It can be said that the COVID-19 pandemic has changed the world. In generic terms, it has changed the world where economic, social, and cultural aspects may find themselves ruptured.

However, as far as medicine and data management are concerned, the COVID-19 pandemic has opened a bleak window of opportunity to allow nations to come together and investigate making a global impact through data sharing, management, and then the application of that management. The world cannot take another pandemic if it were to come any time soon, with the present kind of healthcare structure that stands around most of the world.

It is important to understand the clear role of techniques and technology. The trust factor of these emerging technologies is put to test and will be put to test in future continuously. Appropriate strategic patient data-centric framework and governance need to be created and implemented where innovation with intellect is encouraged.

HDM is assumed to be purely led by technologies like AI and ML but it is not entirely true. At this point, strategic HDM is a combination of strategic thinking, process, and implementation of this strategy using technology. This management is often looked at as purely digital.

At present, there are available tools and technology to create not just a digitized health ecosystem but a smart health ecosystem globally. This can be acquired by strategic HDM which is a combination of strategic roadmap and implementing it using the technology. The challenge is how to use the technology and at what stage in healthcare management, which can help us develop not just a digitized healthcare ecosystem but a smart healthcare ecosystem.

As the world move toward an era of personalization integrated with digitalization, it needs to revolutionize not only digitally but also intellectually. This can be possible if a change of perspective to a mindful patient data-centric approach could be achieved. This strategy is smart and can sustain beyond frequent technological changes.

Digital health ecosystem is possible. Healthcare industries need to aim to create a smart health ecosystem which is now possible than ever. Smart health ecosystem can be created by combining personalization and digitalization.

Understanding the true value of health data types, parsing useful data from a huge data pool, and implementing them to create a smart health ecosystem are the goals of strategic data management. Combining strategic data management with technology can open a billion-dollar market which is yet to be explored.

Strategic HDM is going to not only solve the present big data issue but also create a future roadmap on how well digitalization and personalization can be strategically combined to create a health ecosystem where effective patient care is at the center of the focus.

It is high time to take upon the opportunity and plan better health data management strategies to ensure that the healthcare sectors across the globe take full advantage of digitalization, artificial intelligence, machine learning, and all the other aspects that come as part and parcel of a global healthcare plan—all of this keeping data protectionism in mind.

In a world of ever-changing technology, strategic HDM is the key for success.

References

[1] Federal Communication Commision. February 02, 2017. "Connect America Fund (CAF)." www.fcc.gov/general/connect-america-fund-caf

[2] SELBYVILLE. November 26, 2019. "Substation Automation Market Size to Hit US $207 Billion by 2026." www.newswire.com/news/substation-automation-market-size-to-hit-us-207-billion-by-2026-21041282

[3] Meachem, A. July 27, 2020. "Why Some Rural Communities Lack High-Speed Internet." www.govtech.com/network/why-some-rural-communities-lack-high-speed-internet.html

[4] Health IT.gov. n.d. "United States Core Data for Interoperability (USCDI)." www.healthit.gov/isa/united-states-core-data-interoperability-uscdi

[5] CIO. n.d. "Creating a Data-Driven Culture." www.cio.com/native-link/the-living-enterprise/collection/building-data-driven-business/article/creating-a-data-driven-culture

[6] Prescient & Strategic Intelligence. June 2018. "Propelled by Surge in Demand for Structured and Unstructured Dataset Analysis, Big Data Analytics in Healthcare Market to Surpass $22.7 Billion by 2023." www.psmarketresearch.com/press-release/global-big-data-analytics-in-healthcare-market

[7] World Economic Forum. n.d. "How Much Data is Generated Each Day?" www.weforum.org/agenda/2019/04/how-much-data-is-generated-each-day-cf4bddf29f/

About the Author

Hema Lakkaraju is passionate about her work and is proud of her 12+ years of experience in data-centric, governance, risk, and compliance in the health and life science industry. Her work as an international speaker, blogger, podcaster, and entrepreneur assisted her natural, lateral move into passing on knowledge as an author. Helping others triumph and flourish is a goal of hers, and she's not done yet!

Hema founded HAYAG CORP, an organization dedicated to helping health and life science groups create and effectively implement data-centric compliance and strategic data management framework. As a thought leader and advocate for these topics, she's always pursuing new avenues to spread and share her extensive knowledge. This includes acting as a CISO panelist and international speaker at conferences like IoT world, Secure world, Cyber security, and Cloud Expo. She hopes to encourage others to listen, learn, and adapt to technology so their businesses can not only succeed, but thrive.

Index

OTHER TITLES IN THE HEALTHCARE MANAGEMENT COLLECTION

- *Improv to Improve Healthcare* by Candy Campbell
- *Integrated Delivery* by David Stehlik
- *Mastering Evaluation and Management Services in Healthcare* by Stacy Swartz
- *Lean Thinking for Emerging Healthcare Leaders* by Arnout Orelio
- *Process-Oriented Healthcare Management Systems* by Anita Edvinsson
- *Behind the Scenes of Health Care* by Hesston L. Johnson
- *Predictive Medicine* by Emmanuel Fombu
- *The DNA of Physician Leadership* by Myron J. Beard and Steve Quach
- *Management Skills for Clinicians, Volume II* by Linda R. LaGanga
- *Management Skills for Clinicians, Volume I* by Linda R. LaGanga

Concise and Applied Business Books

The Collection listed above is one of 30 business subject collections that Business Expert Press has grown to make BEP a premiere publisher of print and digital books. Our concise and applied books are for...

- Professionals and Practitioners
- Faculty who adopt our books for courses
- Librarians who know that BEP's Digital Libraries are a unique way to offer students ebooks to download, not restricted with any digital rights management
- Executive Training Course Leaders
- Business Seminar Organizers

Business Expert Press books are for anyone who needs to dig deeper on business ideas, goals, and solutions to everyday problems. Whether one print book, one ebook, or buying a digital library of 110 ebooks, we remain the affordable and smart way to be business smart. For more information, please visit www.businessexpertpress.com, or contact sales@businessexpertpress.com.

www.ingramcontent.com/pod-product-compliance
Lightning Source LLC
Chambersburg PA
CBHW061835220326
41599CB00027B/5288